Our Young Voices

2017

Scholarship Week

Cleveland, Ohio

Banquet
College Fair
Our Young Voices Contest

Our Young Voices 2017, AAMA, Cleveland Scholarshjp Week © 2016 by Universal Prosperity.

Co-Authors:
Jamel Clayton ▪ Taliaha Ward ▪ Jibrael Harris ▪ Asim Shakur-DuVall ▪ Askiya A Shaheed ▪ Cameron Bustamante ▪ Charles Caldwell ▪ Jackson Leach ▪ Sagirah Dillard

All rights reserved. Printed in the United States of America. No part of this book may be used or reproduced in any manner whatsoever without written permission except in the case of brief quotations embodied in critical articles or reviews.

This book is a work of partial non-fiction. However, names, characters, businesses, organizations, places, events and incidents either are the product of the author's imagination or are used fictitiously. Any resemblance to actual persons, living or dead, events, or locales is entirely coincidental.

For information contact: info@uptownmediaventures.com

Book and Cover design by Team Uptown

ISBN: 978-1-68121-072-8

10 9 8 7 6 5 4 3 2 1

Dedicated to enabling youth the experience of expressing themselves with the written word and the

Pride In Authorship!

Table of Contents

Board Chair Preface	7
Introduction	9
Collaborator Statements	11
Endorsements	19
2017 Our Young Voices Essay Winners	33
2016 Our Young Voices Dream Contest Winners	63
The Spoken Word Café Patrick Henry School	77
Coalition For A Better Life, Peace in the Hood	83
Round 1 Boxing. Fitness. Life.	117
The 2016 AAMA Fifth Annual Scholarship Week Banquet, Cleveland, Ohio	119
The 2016, Infinite Scholars College Fair, Cleveland, Ohio	137
Major Supporters and Collaborators	149
Participating Colleges and Universities	157
Summary Reports	171

Cleveland Scholarship Week 2017

Board Chair Preface

As a retired Director of Public Information for the Cleveland Fire Department, I have been involved in many public service activities that benefit the public at large. I have always had a keen desire to positively influence our youth – the future of our society.

As fortuity would have it, I was presented with the idea of starting an initiative for the benefit of our youth. The initiative, ultimately, became the *Pride in Authorship Initiative*. The folks at a small publishing house, *Uptown Media Joint Ventures*, committed to insure the publication of a semi-annual book called *Our Young Voices.*

After much behind the scenes preparation, I am proud to announce the successful publication of a second volume of *Our Young Voices,* in conjunction with the African American Music Association during the Scholarship Week in conjunction with Infinite Scholars.

This is surely just the beginning and we thank all of our sponsors, supporters, and everyone who has contributed to this extremely worthwhile initiative. So please join us, as we celebrate our young essayists who have earned the right to claim the *Pride in Authorship!*

Larry Gray

Board Chairman, Universal Prosperity, Pride in Authorship Initiative

K Kelly with Winston Gragg, President of the African American Music Association and Member of the Infinite Scholars Board of Directors

Introduction

How many people can claim to be published authors as youths?

The *Our Young Voices* publication is one of the manifestations of the *Pride In Authorship Initiative* that seeks to promote written expression by our youth.

Another part of this initiative is the participation in *Youth Literary and Writing Contests*. The winning essays will be published in the *Our Young Voices* publication, with the winner's photo (if available at printing time), and available on major book retailing web sites like Amazon.com and Barnes & Noble.com. Each winner will receive a free copy of their book, an award certification of authorship, along with other prizes!

Yet, ultimately, the greatest reward is seeing their beaming *Pride In Authorship*!

K Kelly McElroy

Technical Director, Universal Prosperity
CEO, Uptown Media Joint Ventures
Author, Best of the Best, Modern Jazz Recordings; Modern Jazz Classics

Cleveland Scholarship Week 2017

Winston Gragg

President African American Music Association and Founder of the Cleveland Scholarship Week

"My idea for being involved with *Our Young Voices* is to make a concentrated effort to helping young people and re-educating adults about today's marketplace. Many adults are afraid of technology, however, our children are not. Walt Disney prepares young children to go to Disney, and we want to prepare kids in elementary and middle school to go to college to get an education. In order to teach young people, you have to get their attention, and that is exactly what *Our Young Voices* is doing."

Dimitrios Kalafatis

Special Events Coordinator
Golden Corral

"Children are our future and I am, personally, proud to support such worthy causes and programs such as Infinite Scholars and the *Our Young Voices* initiative. Golden Corral is committed to the improvement of society-at-large by supporting such noteworthy civic organizations and programs."

Cleveland Scholarship Week 2017

EB Smith

M.P.A., Author, Educator
Media Associate for the
African American Music Association
Vice President, E.B. Smith Project LLC

"Higher education helps develop a person's inner gifts. Student's minds are sharpened with the knowledge and critical thinking skills necessary to compete. I am pleased to be involved with the African American Music Association of Cleveland, Ohio and their continued effort in providing access for young people to get to college. I also support the efforts of *Our Young Voices* in promoting literary expression among our youth. My life serves as proof that their life will be better with it."

Jean Wilson

Executive Administrator
African American Music Association

"*Our Young Voices* gives children and teens an opportunity to express their idea in a public forum. It teaches them how to communicate both written and verbally. Developing these skills at an early age also helps young people to build high self-esteem as well as interpersonal (dealing with others) and intrapersonal communication skills. Students also learn key competencies such as: the ability to solve problems, how to control thoughts and actions, use of critical thinking skills, and the ability to motivate others. We are really excited about the *Our Young Voices* program, because it is making a difference in young people's lives."

Endorsements

Russell Atkins

Carol Shaheed

Judy Jackson-Winston

Harry Boomer

Vince Robinson

Cleveland Scholarship Week 2017

Russell Atkins

(Russell Atkins wearing Cleveland Arts Prize
Lifetime Achievement metal)

> "Our Young Voices is a wonderful opportunity for our youth to express themselves literarily. Such expression is most important to the development of a learned and accomplished community."
>
> Russell Atkins

Russell Atkins is a poet, composer, theorist, editor, and leading literary innovator. He was born on February 25, 1926 in Cleveland, Ohio. He began studying piano at age seven with his mother. From childhood, he exhibited talent in painting, drawing, music, and writing. By age thirteen, he had won several poetry contests. Atkins published his first poem in 1944 in his high school yearbook. With the support of prominent literary figures, Atkins published his poetry in journals and newspapers, including *Experiment* (1947–1951) and the *New York Times* (1951).

Atkins continued his studies of music, performance, and the visual arts through Cleveland College, Cleveland Music School Settlement, Cleveland Institute of Music, Karamu Theatre, and Cleveland School of Art. This musical training is a key to Atkins's poetic style since musical structures are central in his writing.

In 1950, Atkins cofounded what is probably the oldest black-owned literary magazine, *Free Lance*, a publication of avant-garde writing that contributed to the development of New American poetry. He created a style of concrete poetry in which visual presentation of words on the page predominates. He experimented stylistically with the extreme use of the apostrophe, embedding of words within words, and use of continuous words.

In the mid-1950s, he began utilizing an abstract technique he called "phenomenalism," which juxtaposed unfamiliar and familiar elements. Atkins advocated using the imagination "to exploit range, to create a body of effect, event, colors, characteristics, moods, verbal stresses pushed to a maximum." He did not try to make his work comprehensible to casual readers but strove for dense complexity of meaning.

While in his 90s Russell Atkins finally has started to get the recognition he so richly deserves. In 2017, an anthology *In The Company of Russell Atkins* was published in his honor. Atkins also, won the Cleveland Arts Prized for Lifetime Achievement and had a portion of Grand Avenue in Cleveland, Ohio renamed to: Russell Atkins Way, Grand Avenue.

(Russell Atkins being awarded "Russell Atkins Way" street sign by Mayor Frank Jackson, standing left, along with original Muntu Poet M.A. Shaheed, standing right)

Carol Shaheed

As a retired history teacher of 36 years and a master's degree in education from Cleveland State University, I am well aware of the importance of our children having the needed skills to read and have their particular voices heard.

By establishing and designing courses such as Black Awareness and Black Biographies, accepted by the state board of education for the East Cleveland school system, allowed my students the opportunity to write and express feeling unique to the black experience.

"Our Young Voices Initiative provides the same opportunities for students to express their uniqueness and I believe that this program allows students to showcase their talents in a productive environment."

Carol Shaheed

Judy Jackson-Winston

JJ Winston has worked in the area of Behavioral Health for over 20 years and is now employed as a Family Court Magistrate Judge in Cleveland, Ohio. JJ Winston is licensed as an Independent Social Worker and Attorney in the state of Ohio.

An avid reader whose hobbies include fishing, watching movies, writing fiction stories and spending time with family and friends. The Anniversary is JJ Winston's first novel.

> "I love the fact that our young people have a chance to express themselves in a literary sense and to become a published co-author."
>
> JJ Winston

Harry Boomer

"My experience in journalism and the media has proven to me how important the ability to express oneself is, both through the spoken and written word. I support the critical aims of Our Young Voices in offering our youth the inspiration, encouragement, and vehicle to make their literary expressions come true as published co-authors."

Harry Boomer

Harry Boomer's broadcasting career began in Washington, D.C., where he was a Disco Jock, an on-air personality, music director, talk show host and served in various other management positions, including two stints as a news director (United Broadcasting and Radio One).

Boomer came to Ohio in 1988 to manage and program WBXT-AM in Canton, Ohio. He also worked in public television at WEAO/WNEO-TV in Kent, Ohio and volunteered at WVIZ-TV 25 Idea Stream in Cleveland.

While covering assignments for WOIO/WUAB on a part-time basis in the early 1990s, he was heard regularly on WCPN-90.3 FM, Cleveland the NPR affiliate, where he served as assistant news director. He was also a reporter, producer and major contributor to NPR. Boomer debuted a statewide news magazine program entitled *Infohio* for the radio station. Boomer took a full time reporter position at channels 19 and 43 WOIO/WUAB and is currently an anchor/reporter and talk show host for the stations. Boomer received the Silver Circle Award in 2015 from the National Academy of Television Arts & Sciences/NATAS, a distinction given for at least 25 years in television.

Boomer is the president of the Greater Cleveland Association of Black Journalist/GCABJ. Twice during Boomer's leadership, the chapter has been named the NABJ Professional Chapter of the Year, most recently in 2016. He is a valued member of the editorial board of Cleveland 19 and CLE 43 in Cleveland, Ohio. He is the executive producer and host of CLE 43 Focus, a weekly, half-hour public affairs show. In 2014 Boomer was named a HistoryMaker and an oral video of his life's story is part of a permanent archive at the Library of Congress. He was named in 2016 as president of the Cleveland Police Athletic League and to the board the Historic League Park in the Hough community of Cleveland. He has served on the boards of the Ohio Associated Press, The Ohio Center for Broadcasting, First Tee Cleveland, the Citizens Committee on AIDS/HIV, the North East Ohio Health Services Board of Directors. He served a member of the Continuing Education Committee at Cleveland State University.

Vince Robinson

    Vince Robinson is a Cleveland-based arts advocate involved in a number of pursuits involving media and communication. A 1980 graduate of Kent State University, he initially began as a radio news reporter covering local politics for WKNT-radio. His radio news career included stints at WHLO-AM 640 in Akron, WJMO-1490AM and WERE-1300AM, both in Cleveland. He presently co-hosts 360 Info Network on AM1490-WERE. Additionally, he is the host and co-producer of *Open Door*, a television talk show airing on Cable9 in Summit County, Ohio.

Robinson is also a musician. His group, Vince Robinson & The Jazz Poets, was founded in 1997 with now Cleveland City Councilman Kevin Conwell (drums) and *Horns-N-Things* bassist Derrick James. He plays keys in the Latin soul fusion group *Timbara* and the reggae group *Yardstar*.

In 2016, he and business partner Randy Norfus opened Larchmere Arts, a full-service photography studio, art gallery and performance venue. The business is emerging as a cultural institution in the Larchmere Art district of Cleveland. In addition to music events, cultural activities including lectures and meetings are facilitate in the space. The works of multicultural artists has been featured in the gallery, including paintings, photographs and sculptures.

As a photographer, his work has been shown in galleries and other public spaces. Most recently, a collection of images taken in the West African nation of Ghana was displayed in the Umbajii Gallery at Kent State University. A collection of images of recording artists from several genres was hung in the Shinn House Gallery in Cleveland during the winter of 2017.

Currently, he is serving on a committee to address the needs of African American artists pursuing funding by Cuyahoga Arts and Culture for individual artist grants. He will also be serving on the board of Heights Arts, a non-profit organization serving the arts community of Cleveland Heights, Ohio.

He is a published author, having completed his first book "*Got Words?*" (Parablist Publishing House) in 2015. In partnership with Uptown Media Joint Ventures, his publishing imprint, Sankofa Freedom Press, launched in 2017.

"Our Young Voices is a great opportunity to give inspiration to our young people by celebrating their literary expressions."

Vince Robinson

2017
Our Young Voices Essay Winners

Cleveland, Ohio

Askiya A Shaheed
Cameron Bustamante
Charles Caldwell
Jackson Leach
Sagirah Dillard

Author Asim Shakur-DuVall

Age 13

Cleveland Scholarship Week 2017

Five Years of Luck

Five years. Five years of tanks and heavily armed men roaming the streets. Five years of the King's soldiers dying. Five years ended with the King dropping to his knees in front of the head government agent. With the soldiers who had fought for the King jailed and killed off day by day. As I sat on the cool leather couch of our home this is what was passing through my mind. This and one other notion... We got lucky. We could've easily been slaughtered by the Apato government agents. We could have been killed just as our fellow Tico soldiers had been. Shot and forgotten. So I merely had to look outside the window at the remaining dead bodies to remember how lucky we were.

"Mark," my mother spoke to me in a soft voice. Her voice faltered and quivered and inside my heart was pounding. I didn't want my mother to cry. "Your father and I have decided to," she stopped. I felt like reassuring her that everything was ok. But alas, it wasn't. Finally, my father's deep voice finished her sentence with a heavy sigh, "We have decided to join the resistance."

My heart skipped a beat at the sound of those gut wrenching words. Even though the war was over, fighting continued in small pockets between the resistance and the government. I imagined the hundreds of resistance captives cramped into a tiny cell. I couldn't bring myself to imagine them amongst the suffering captives.

Everyone in my life whom I loved had died except for my parents. My beloved Uncle Sam was gone. My grandpa and grandma had been killed by shrapnel. And even now my cousin Tom was locked up in a dingy cell awaiting death. Then it reoccurred to me again. We were lucky. I managed to conjure up a few words to break the displeasing silence, "When will you be leaving?"

My father looked up, and for a split second I thought I saw sorrow and a hint of fear in his eyes. He solemnly spoke, "We joined a few weeks ago. That is why we have been gone for majority of the day and most of the nights. They have told us that we must pack our bags and start living in the resistance camps. So this is a final goodbye."

I couldn't cry. I had to show that I was strong enough to survive on my own. I have access to the house and the market a few blocks away. I would survive alone. I was Mark Johnson, heir to Mary and Lucas Johnson.

I must have been radiating determination and pride because when I looked up, I saw my parents beaming down at me. I smiled back just as proudly. This was a moment I will never forget. It was the best moment we could've possibly shared despite the utter destruction happening beyond the cozy confinement of our home.

A heavy pounding on the door interrupted our peaceful moment. My father rose from his seat perplexed. He strode to the door just as it was smashed in with a vicious kick. Splinters flew every which way. Glass shards lashed at my skin like needles. My father raised his fists to strike at a looming figure but was gunned down by three other ruthless men. My mother screamed for me to run. She was gagged and knocked unconscious. She fell, crumpled and feeble. My father yelled for me to run but he suffered the same fate as my mother. I knew they weren't dead. But I couldn't leave them to the hands of the government. I was bubbling over with rage.

The remaining men then turned to me. I looked up in panic. Then I ran. I ran and smashed right through the back window, oblivious to the blood streaming from my gashed arms. I heard feet pounding after me. I knew I could outrun them with their heavy boots and gear. My fear was their weapons. I made a quick decision that saved my life. I turned to the shed, just as a barrage of gun shells dropped down to the dirt. The bullets hit the ground, kicking up enough dust to obscure my figure for a few moments.

As the guards tried to clear their vision, I ducked into the shadows of the shed. I grabbed for the nearest tool and found myself holding a pickaxe. I would have mobility and stealth, but virtually no range. I prepared for the worst. I was only sixteen years old with plans for the life ahead of me. I would not go down like this. But the main question in my head was, *'Could I bring myself to kill?'*

One of the guards whistled a staggered tune. And out of seemingly nowhere came the largest wolf beast my eyes ever saw. To call it a wolf would be an understatement. As it took its position next to the guard, I saw that it rose to the guard's rib cage and had layers of teeth. Its sharp claws could strike fear in the eyes of men. Its expression said it all; *It would kill without thinking.* I knew at that moment that I faced an impossible situation. I told myself, 'I *will die either way. I might as well go down with a fight.'* I ran out making no attempt to conceal my presence. I pulled back my arm and swung at the nearest guard. My stickball skills were put to some use. He fell to the ground dead on impact. I forced myself to turn away. The remaining guard was replacing the clip in his gun when he was bashed in the back of the head with my bloodstained weapon. I thought I was done but then I heard the angry snarl of the beast looking me in the eye. I dropped the weapon and gave in to my inevitable fate.

The brute stared at me and instead of killing me, he sat down. I realized that it had no intent to kill me. I reached out a nervous hand, hoping he wouldn't bite it off. He jumped on me and licked my face. I laughed and sat up, wiping the viscus saliva off my sweaty face.

As I played with my newfound friend, I smelled smoke. To my horror I realized our home was in a blaze. I couldn't hold it in. I wept and wept to my heart's content. My home, my parents. I needed to leave before the rest of the agents came back to look for the two they had sent. I stared down at their lifeless bodies and an outrageous thought formed in my mind. I would end the reign of the Apato government. Glaring at their dead bodies with my home ablaze, I pondered if I could do this to the rest of the agents. I saw my parents tied in the back of a government truck and I made a decision. It wasn't a matter of can I do it - it was simply when.

I scrounged the corpses for useful tools. I took the first guard's leather belt from around his cold waist and tied it around my own. I now had a dagger, flashlight, and a tear gas quietly clinking together whenever I moved. Additional search yielded nothing except for some extra ammo. Then I stared at the weapon I dreaded the most. His gun. The shiny green weapon glinted in the moonlit sky. I couldn't take down the whole government with a pickaxe - that was certain. But I was never a violent person so handling a gun would cause me much inner conflict. I struggled with myself for a moment but my intellect won over my self-conscience. I scooped up the full automatic gun and slung it over my shoulder. I then let my gaze drift to the other guard who lay limp with a gash in the back of his head.

I walked over to him until I heard someone shout, "He's right there!"

I darted my face up and saw, sprinting towards me, six more agents' guns trained at my head. I hefted the agent onto the back of the beast that still sat obediently and ran.

I must've run for hours because when I stopped and regained my senses, I was on the outskirts of Tyco. It was around dawn so I figured that I should rest my bones for a while. I sat with my aching legs stretched out and my back propped up against a tall oak tree. I looked at the guard slumped on the creature's shoulders and realized that the 'creature' needed a name.

I whistled for it mimicking the tune of the slain guard and it was soon at my side. I looked over it for a moment and then said, "Nova. Nova sounds like a good name."

Nova vigorously wagged his thick clumpy tail. I heard a rumble coming from my stomach. I realized how hungry I was so I got up with a heavy groan. Nevertheless, I fought through my pain. With gun in hand, I strode off into the dense foliage with Nova rambunctiously tramping through the woods. Suddenly my ears picked up a rustling from the bushes nearby. Nova made a vicious growl and bared his pointed teeth. I silently gave myself a countdown. *3...2...1.* I dashed into the bushes with lighting speed and my foot tapped something. I reached down and a girl leaped out of the bushes. I aimed my gun at her head. Her eyes surprisingly showed no fear. Instead they showed anger and utter resentment. Nova came padding to my side. He glared at the girl with just the same feelings as she mirrored to me.

I grunted out, "Who are you to try and sneak up on me?"

"I don't have to answer to you," she retorted.

"Then you shall die," and as soon as the words came out of my mouth I knew I wouldn't. Never. I was not a murderer. I wouldn't kill an innocent human, unless they were an agent. It seemed she read my thoughts.

"You... no, you wouldn't. You can't. You're too afraid."

I tossed my gun to the side and helped the girl up. She had auburn hair with hazel brown eyes. Her face was petite along with her straight nose. She wore a green tank top with black jeans. She had a brave and strong persona that couldn't be broken.

"We should probably try again," she spoke with less of an I- want-to-slit- your- throat tone.

"Yeah," I said, "we should. My name is Mark Johnson. What's yours?"

"I'm Julie Coffman," she replied. "I was just trying to see if you were an agent or not."

I realized I did slightly look like one with my belt and gun.

I told her, "No. This is my wolf beast Nova. We are planning to save Tico by slaying the head agent," I stammered trying not to go with a direct approach, "We could use some extra help."

Julie's eyes lit up with joy, "Yes, I can help you!"

I said, "Ok but first you'll need this." I shoved the dead guard off Nova's back and tossed her his gun and belt. She snatched the gun out of the air and without hesitation, slung it over her shoulder. She then looped the belt through her tight jeans.

"We'll need some training," I remarked.

She replied seriously, "Agreed."

So we trained. We sharpened our knives from the belts and turned them into sharp glistening daggers. The jagged curves in the silvery steel were like no other. We stripped the clothes off the perished men and stuffed dead grass and weeds inside them to make hodgepodge targets. They helped each day we practiced. Each time we tried a new tactic, whether it was stealth or brute strength. We polished our knife throwing skills. We started off implying our knives in nearby trees. But after weeks of practice, we had enough skill to put sharpshooters to shame. Our newly muscular arms would impale the limp dummies with a sharp blade. We also stuffed tree bark into the barrels of our guns to silence the sound. What used to be a volley of rambunctious bangs came the sound of a dry cough. We couldn't practice much on our shooting seeing that we had only a limited amount of ammo. So we cut the tops from fallen acorns and practiced with those. Nova however needed no training. He was the same size as a bear on four paws and had twice the viciousness.

Soon we were ready to fight. Our last day of training ended with a lap around the makeshift track we created with stones. When Julie and I crossed the finish line at the same time we knew we were ready.

As I sat panting around our fire I said, "Let's go over our plan."

Julie looked up at me and answered, "Sure let's do it."

Our plan was simple but dangerous. We would first have to toss all evidence of our camp into the river not far from where we were. Then at daybreak we would furtively tiptoe through the woods until we were spit out into the town. From there, we would join in on one of the hostage groups marching toward the base led by heavily armed guards. We would have to leave our guns in the river, for this part of the plan required our dagger skills. Then as we marched to the dungeon below the government base, we would kill our two guards and head to the main room unseen. It was a very risky plan but we had to do it. Nova would be our back up. He would use his keen senses to tell us if there are upcoming agents.

As I rattled all of this off to Julie, I felt proud of myself. I had single handedly made this plan. It would work. We looked up into the sky and decided to get a few hours of sleep. As I dozed off, I had a sudden feeling of peace that I hadn't felt in a long time.

I was abruptly awoken from my slumber by a rough shaking. I looked up to see Julie standing over me.

"It's almost dawn and you weren't up," she explained. "I didn't want you to oversleep."

"Thanks," I said drowsily.

We began our perilous trek out of the woods. Nova was constantly on the lookout for danger, but there was none until we reached the town.

As soon as I saw the town, I remembered many good memories of it, but they were short-lived for ahead were a group of captives. I jerked my head toward Julie; we both nodded to each other and advanced upon the throng.

As we inched closer, I realized the scope of what we were trying to pull off. We were trying to break into a highly secured area and bring down the most powerful man in the world. At that moment my confidence swayed. As we slipped into the crowd, Nova pretended to be watching us as to not raise suspicion. As we walked and got nearer to the base, I was scared that our plan would fail. When we reached a large corridor, I glanced to Julie.

It was time. The guards split us into ten groups with two guards for every group. Julie and I were in group A and Nova came and padded along glaring at us to keep up the rouse. We darted from our lines, drew our knives, and killed the guards. I thought to myself, *'That makes three.'* The captives stared and thanked us gratefully.

But we had no time to lose. I darted off with Julie and Nova on my heels. I had no idea where I was going. I was just following my instincts. I saw a sign saying Judgment Hall. I burst through the door and saw two people in chains with a man standing over them.

The man spoke, "Julie and Mark. I've been expecting you. I've been informed of your plans from my spies who overheard your conversations. You have arrived faster than I had anticipated. I'm Julius, the head agent. Come join me as your parents get sentenced to death."

Julie and I slowly stepped forward. I took in the surroundings of the grand room. Two guards stood straight-backed on either side of Julius. They were like Native Americans, their faces were blank without expression or emotion and they were loyal to their King. There was another wolf beast sitting next to the guards. Nova growled at it and bared his sharp teeth. I was bubbling with so much rage that I forgot our initial plan to kill Julius. I darted toward my parents and slashed at their chains with all my strength. The chains clattered to the floor. Then I heard a scream. I turned and saw Julie being dragged away.

"Julie!" I shouted.

"Go Mark Go!" she yelled back.

As I ran I shouted to her, "I will come back for you Julie! I promise."

We ran and ran out of the base. Out of the town. Deep into the woods. I flopped to the ground exhausted and embraced my parents. We got lucky. Julie however didn't. Although Julius still lived, with my parents to help me, we could build a better and stronger resistance. I knew that this was the beginning of a new age. Tyco would be restored to its long lost splendor.

Smart is Cool!

Author Askiya A Shaheed

Age 13

Cleveland Scholarship Week 2017

My Hero

My hero is my grandfather because he teaches me things that my father doesn't teach me. My grandfather also teaches me very important lessons. He and my father are the only reason why I'm a good Muslim. Because if it wasn't for my grandfather I wouldn't know half the stuff that I know today.

My grandfather is also the imam of my masjid, which means leader, so he manages the mosque to make sure that the masjid is in fine condition. I don't know what I would do without my grandfather.

Maybe I wouldn't have the same guidance without him. I hope my grandfather can live long enough for me to grow up and to see his great grandchildren; so that when I grow up I can give them the best example of good people and a good Muslim - just like my grandfather did for me.

Author Cameron Bustamante

Age 12

Cleveland Scholarship Week 2017

Cameron's Journal

(Four Short Essays)

Dragon Land

Once upon a time there was a knight. He always wanted to see a dragon but King Dan said, "No he can't see a dragon because he is not brave." The knight thought he was brave because he killed a dinosaur in a castle before.

When it was night time he went to Dragon Land. He saw a king dragon in his home with two little dragons and a mother. He was so happy he said, "Hello dragon can you take me on a ride?" The king dragon sang and said, "Get on my back, I am taking you to the castle. The knight got on his back and the dragon took off. When they arrived at the castle the dragon landed. The castle was big and it was blue. The dragon took the knight in the castle and sang, "Do you want to stay at the castle." All of the sudden King Dan came in the castle and said, "Go back to my castle!" The knight said, "Bye" and went back to the castle.

The knight was so mad at the king he went to the king and said, "I am going back to the Dragon Land." When the knight got out of the castle the king trapped him in a net. The knight cut the net with his sword and ran to his horse and went to the Dragon Land. When the knight arrived he went to the king dragon. When the knight told him about what happen to him he called all the dragons to plan an attack on King Dan. King Dan was also planning an attack on the king dragon.

When it was night the king dragon went to see King Dan. When he arrived at King Dan's castle he went to King Dan and said, "All of the dragons are going to attack you in five minutes you better be ready!"

When it five minutes passed all the dragons got ready and King Dan got ready. They both came at a stop in the battle field. Both kings said, "Attack!" They fought until there were until two were standing. Then they played rock, paper, and seizer until one won. The king dragon won the war. All the dragons and knights got to be friend.

Gingerbread Soccer Player

Once upon a time there was a 25 year old coach. He needed a new soccer player. So one day he made a gingerbread soccer player one yard high. He made the gingerbread man's eyes out of candy, his nose out of cookies, and his shirt, pants, and shoes out of frosting.

When he was done he put the gingerbread soccer player into the oven. When it was done he took the gingerbread soccer player out the oven. All of the sudden the gingerbread man jump out and said, "Run! Run as fast as you can! You can't catch me I am the gingerbread man!" So away he went.

When the gingerbread man got out the house he met a referee. "Stop, stop!" said the referee, "We want to eat you." The gingerbread man laughed and said, "Run! Run as fast as you can! You can't catch me I am the gingerbread man!" So away he went.

When the gingerbread man came to a stop he met soccer players. "Stop! Stop!" said the soccer players, "We want to eat you!" The gingerbread man laughed, "I ran away from the coach, the referee and I can run away from you to!"

The gingerbread man ran faster than ever and said, "Run! Run as fast as you can! You can't catch me I am the gingerbread man!" So away he went.

When he came to a town he saw soccer fans. "Stop! Stop we want to eat you!" said the soccer fans. The gingerbread man laughed and said, "Run! Run as fast as you can! You can't catch me I am the gingerbread man!"

Then he saw kids. "Stop! Stop we want to eat you!" The gingerbread men said, "Run! Run as fast as you can! You can't catch me I am the gingerbread man!"

When the gingerbread man came to a soccer ball. He said, "Can you help me?" The soccer ball said, "Yes," and laughs. He took him into a little gingerbread room and closed the door. Then he ate him. He ate him in 1 minute.

Ho, ho, boo!

Ho, ho, boo! Let's take a look at two great holidays - Christmas and Halloween. Do you have a preference between the two? I will show you how they are similar, different and then reveal my favorite holiday of the two.

Christmas and Halloween have a lot of similarities. There is always a lot of delicious food; especially candy. On both Halloween and

Christmas there is a lot of decorating of your home and yard; even cookies.

On Halloween and Christmas you can watch lots of movies made specifically for that holiday. There is even one movie that celebrates Halloween and Christmas. It's called the *Nightmare Before Christmas*.

As much as Christmas and Halloween are alike there are also a number of differences. Christmas is a religious holiday and is celebrated at home, with family and sometimes the church. Halloween is celebrated out on the street ringing other people's doorbell for candy. With Christmas you choose to dress up and wear nice clothes, whereas on Halloween you may wear a costume.

I would pick Christmas as my favorite holiday because I can give my family gifts and they can give me gifts too. And I get to see all my family. That is why I like Christmas as my favorite holiday.

In conclusion I have compared and contrasted two of my favorite holidays. I finished up by picking Christmas as my favorite holiday and explained why I like it so much. Do you have a favorite holiday?

Sports or Good Grades

This report is about student doing sports and not caring about school, or students going to school, and getting good grades.

School is about learning. Everything else should come second. It's wrong that kids can coast through school without learning much. This rule will make kids work harder to get a good education. Anyway, it's hard to become a professional athlete. People need something to fall back on. And if someone does go pro, they'll still need to know how to read and do math.

Sport and grades have nothing to do with each other. A kid can become a great athlete - nothing should stand in their way. And even if some kids have no chance of going pro, they shouldn't be punished for their grades. Think of everything you learn from sports: teamwork, fast thinking, discipline, and other skills. There are a lot of things you need to know to survive in the world and you can't learn them all from books.

In my opinion I think getting good grades is more important because if you get bad grades you won't get a job and a house.

That is why a student should stay in school and get A's, B's, or C's before they play sports.

What do you think?

Author Charles Caldwell
Age 18

Cleveland Scholarship Week 2017

life

the beauty of life
(and by that I mean the ugliness)
is that, for the life of me,
she couldn't see
the difference
between a diamond
and a piece of glass
she could not distinguish
the perfect pitch
from the usual sounds
and so, I waited
for the car
to accelerate
to hit a bumpy road
it finally did
but when it was over
we had lost *each other*
in the broken glass
and noise

Author Jackson Leach
Age 10

The Dragon Slayer

Once upon a time there was a 10-year-old boy named Tyler. He was fascinated with the village dragon slayer Xangar and wanted to be just like him. He watched the dragon slayer every day until he decided that it was what he wanted to be - a dragon slayer.

So he started working at a hotdog stand to save up money for dragon slaying lessons, weapons, and armor. After five months of saving money he started to train with the master Xangar. After that he decided to climb up the mountain where the dragon Vecko lived.

When Tyler started to climb the mountain, Xangar stopped him and told him that he cannot kill the dragon. Xangar explained that Vecko was his brother. Tyler asked how this was possible and Xangar explained to Tyler that Vecko was trying to kill a witch named Furo that was killing the people of the village. So Vecko challenged Furo to a battle and right when Vecko stabbed Furo, Furo cast a spell that turned Vecko into a dragon.

Tyler got really worried and did not listen to Xangar because he knew he had to kill Vecko to save the villagers. When Tyler climbed the mountain he instantly saw Vecko and then realized that Vecko was innocent.

Vecko told Tyler that Furo survived the stab and was living on the other side of the mountain. So Vecko and Tyler decided to team up against Furo, the witch, and destroy her after all. Tyler hopped on Vecko's back and flew to the other side of the mountain to find Furo.

When they found Furo, the witch tried to stop them with a spell but Vecko froze the witch with his ice breath. Furo was too powerful and broke this ice. Vecko realized the witch was too strong for both of them and they needed to come up with a plan.

Tyler decided to pull out his sword and Vecko put an ice shield around Tyler to protect him. Furo was caught off guard and Tyler had a chance to stab the witch again this time with the power of dragon ice to make sure she would die for good.

After Tyler and Vecko were done battling the witch, they decided to partner up and become a monster battling team. Once the villagers found out Furo was dead and Vecko was innocent, they celebrated all night and had a big feast.

Vecko and Tyler saved the villagers and the day! They travelled around the world saving villages and they became best friends.

Our Young Voices

Author Sagirah Dillard
Age 14

Cleveland Scholarship Week 2017

The World Today

Sometimes I question where life goes

The people I see, what I know

I myself, don't care for wealth

But in this world, you only have yourself

May I ask what perfection is?

I need to sit down and clear this deception

Let me ask, is it what society thinks?

But society's head is way in the sink

I wish I could drift off like a blossom or like a petal from a rose

Getting away from life's bumpy roads

Only if I could find that note

Just to see all life wrote

I wish I was quiet and in the background

It seems like my name is getting around

I'm not saying that's a bad thing you know

People will talk about you wherever you go

Something inside me makes me speak

My mind lying to my heart, which is always deceived

I think today's problem is that we are all the same

If we were different we might all keep sane

Now let's take a long look at the world, do you see what I see?

The world we live in main word is me

Our Young Voices Dream Contest
2016 Winners
African American Music Association

Cleveland, Ohio

The Our Young Voices, Dream Contest for Middle Schools was held on Saturday, September 10, 2016 at the First Cleveland Mosque.

The winners of the Our Young Voices Dream Contest are:

Jamel Clayton

Taliaha Ward

Jibrael Harris

Cleveland Scholarship Week 2017

Author Jamel Clayton
Age 14

Why I Want To Go To College

I want to go to college because I want to be successful and prove society wrong. As a young black man everything is against us. I have something to prove to myself. I have to be a leader and encouragement to my community and race. I want to go to the Marines, then I want to go to college. I want to get my masters and doctorate degrees. I want everyone to see that I am independent and that I can be successful. My education is the most important thing in my life. I want other young Blacks to do the same and to have the same mind-set, persistence, and determination. A house divided can't stand. Divided we fall. Abraham Lincoln wrote with unity there is strength, united we stand for the strength of the wolf is the pack and the strength of the pack is the wolf.

Cleveland Scholarship Week 2017

Author Talaiha Ward
Age 14

Why I Want To Go To College

I want to go to college because I want to get a good education. An education will benefit me in multiple ways. People with an education tend to get better jobs than people without an education.

Another reason I would like to go to college is because I want to set an example for my younger siblings. My younger siblings look up to me. If I don't go to college, there is a 64% chance they won't either.

I also want to go to college to pursue my career as a neurosurgeon. To become a neurosurgeon, I have to go to college for six to eight years. If I don't go to college, this won't happen.

Also, I would make more money going to college. I want to make enough to afford my own house, car, bills, and essentials for my family. And maybe build my own hospital someday.

There are excellent reasons to go to college including: to get an education, to be an example for someone that looks up to you, to get the job that you want instead of flipping burgers, and to make enough money to live long and prosper.

Cleveland Scholarship Week 2017

Author Jibreal Harris
Age 14

Why I Want To Go To College

Going to college is important to me because it is a way to make my dreams come true. I dream of becoming a commercial pilot. I want to fly all over the world. I want to see different places and meet different people. When I see planes flying over me I think that, 'someday I will fly one of those.' To travel to different places and to see the world would be very expensive but if you are a pilot you get paid to see all these great places. Going to college and studying aviation for four years will help me become a pilot. When I am at college I will have flight training to help me get the flight certificates and training that I will need. Even though no college is required to be a pilot, I think it is important to have a college degree.

Cleveland Scholarship Week 2017

Our Young Voices

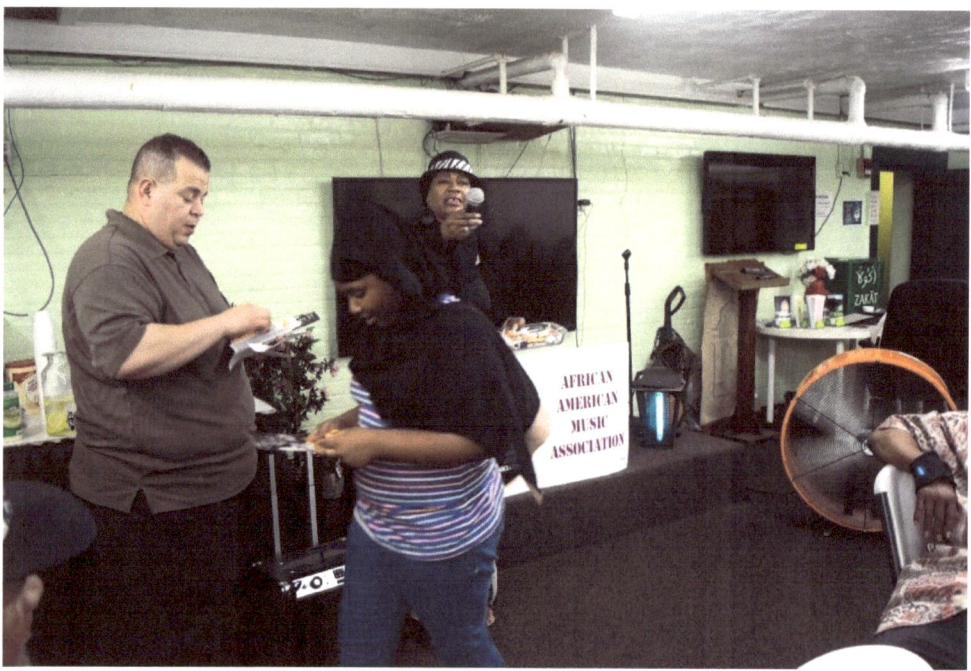

(Dimitrios Kalafatis, Special events Marketing Coordinator, Golden Corral, top left; bottom, left)

Cleveland Scholarship Week 2017

(Imam Abbas, top; and Jean Wilson, AAMA, bottom)

Cleveland Scholarship Week 2017

Our Young Voices

Cleveland Scholarship Week 2017

The Spoken Word Cafe

Patrick Henry School
Cleveland, Ohio

The Spoken Word Cafe was held Thursday, November 10, 2016 at the Patrick Henry School. The event was supported by City of Cleveland Councilman, Kevin Conwell; Mrs. Yvonne Conwell, Cuyahoga County Council Representative; Universal Prosperity, Uptown Media Joint Ventures, along with many others.

The main attraction was all the young Spoken Word artists who all were eighth grade students. The various renditions were performed in spirited and eloquent fashions.

The students were joined by various staff in poetic expressions, including Ms. B. Anderson, the Aspiring Principal, along with other staff members.

Other highlights included an upbeat musical presentation by Kevin Conwell and the Footprints Band. Also, uplifting statements were made by various Patrick Henry staff including: Principal, Mrs. M. Martin; Aspiring Principal, Ms. B. Anderson; Assistant Principal, Mr. R. Shaw; and Dean of Engagement, Mr. M. Jester.

This publication certainly is another representation of the dedication to inspiring our youth and service in the community.

Cleveland Scholarship Week 2017

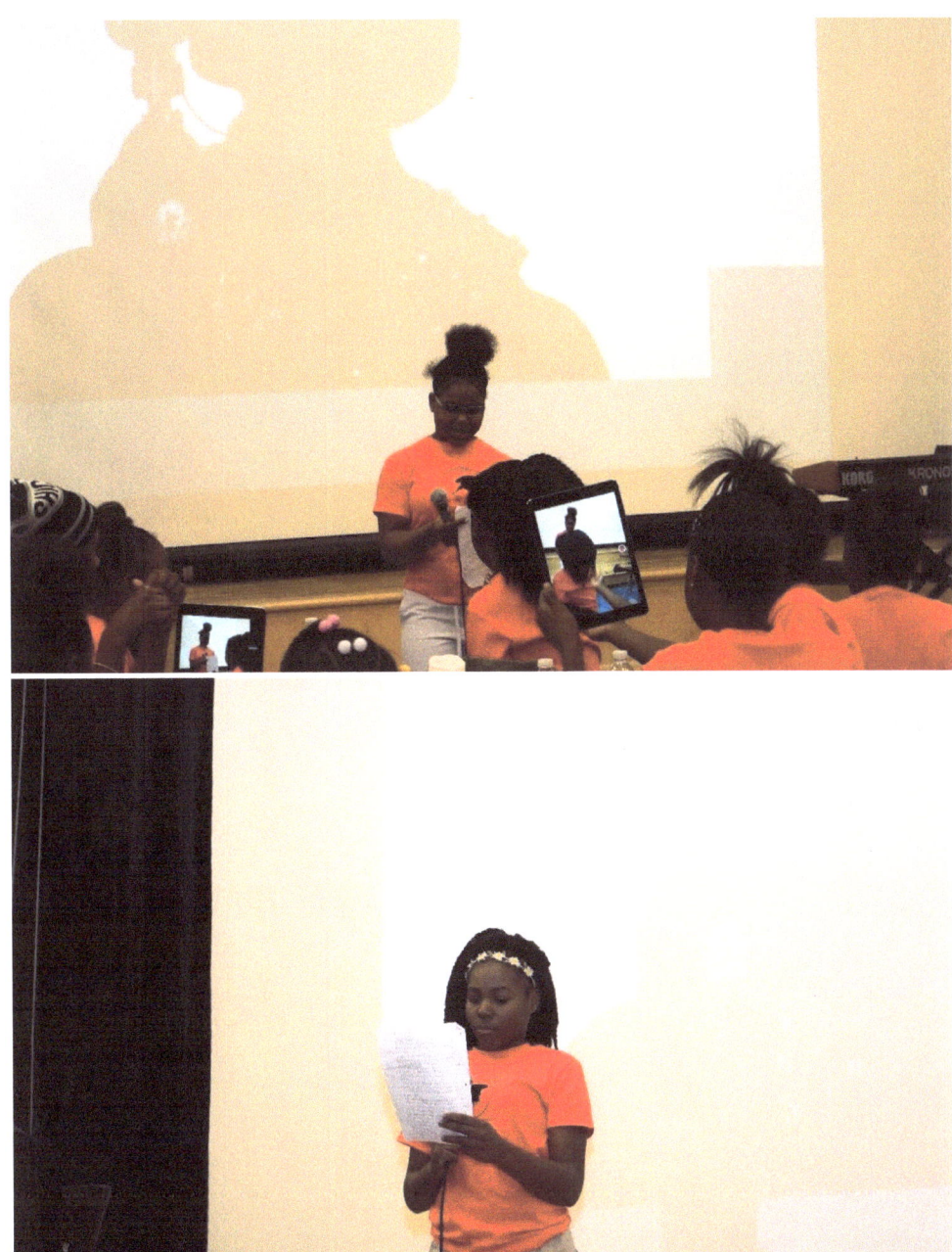

Our Young Voices

Cleveland Scholarship Week 2017

Our Young Voices

Cleveland Scholarship Week 2017

Coalition For A Better Life, Peace In The Hood

Amir El-Hajj Khalid A. Samad

El Hajj Amir Khalid A. Samad is an internationally known and recognized community activist and leader who formerly served as the Assistant to the Public Safety Director for the City of Cleveland for youth gang intervention. He has also served as a Gang Prevention and Investigative Specialist for the Cleveland Board of Education Gang Task Force. In addition, he is Chief Executive Officer and Co-Founder of Coalition for A Better Life, dba Peace in the Hood, Inc., an organization dedicated to Peace, Justice and Empowerment and also serves as a spokesperson for the International (Formerly National) Council for Urban (Formations) Peace, Justice and Empowerment.

As an internationally acclaimed specialist on urban violence, youth empowerment and gang intervention, Amir Samad has lectured throughout the nation and has appeared on national radio and television shows such as Tavis Smiley, Nightline, Keeping It Real with Rev. Al Sharpton, The Warren Ballentine Show and PBS as a leading authority on these issues. He has served as a convener for the International Council (formerly National   Council) Urban (Formations) Peace and Justice Leadership Summits.

In 1987, Khalid Samad, the late Omar Ali-Bey and other community leaders formed The Coalition For A Better Life which addressed the myriad of challenges facing urban America: racism, drugs, gang violence, police corruption, miseducation and an absence of leadership just to name a few. This unified coalition of faith and community based groups involved Muslims, Christians, Jews, Hebrew Israelites , liberals, conservatives, civil rights activists, and community activists, as well as cultural nationalists. This rainbow coalition was inclusive of all ethnic groups and nationalities. This level of cooperation, under Muslim Leadership, was uunprecedented in America given this country's history of inter-religious relations. The Coalition was recognized as a national model for crime prevention and intervention.

The Coalition For A Better Life designed and implemented five monumental projects that were nationally acclaimed. These projects were: 1) Community Empowerment Drug Patrols (which were 24 hours a day, 7 days a week and involved street engagement of violent drug dealers as well as assisting them to cross over into productive life styles by dealing with dealer addiction issues; 2) Rites of Passage, 3) Mentoring (Project A.D.A.M.), 4) Entrepreneurship (Project Ujima) and 5) Cultural Empowerment (Hip Hop exchange which included such nationally known rap artists as Public Enemy, and X-Clan as well as nationally known spoken word artists, The Last Poets).   These initiatives together formed Cleveland's first *Community Empowerment*

Project. The notorious King Kennedy Housing Estates was averaging 3 homicides and shootings a week during this time. The efforts of The Coalition for a Better Life sparked a multimillion dollar infusion of improvements and services into King Kennedy and throughout the other housing estates in Cleveland.

Khalid A. Samad is a leading authority on cross-cultural relations, one of the most important religious and cultural diversity issues of our time. He has worked as a member of the City of Cleveland's Arab-American Concerns Committee, established after several robberies and shootings took place in Arab-American owned stores.

In December of 2008, Amir Samad was asked to be one of the panelists in Washington, D.C. at a youth violence summit sponsored by Rep. Bobby Scott of Virginia. On May 7, 2009, he again spoke on youth violence at the Youth Promise Act Day on the Hill. In 2008, 100 Black Men honored (Khalid Samad) as one of the Five Outstanding Cleveland Leaders.

On September 17, 2011, he spoke at a workshop during the Congressional Black Caucus Weekend. In 2012, he was named as one of the Community Heroes by the Plain Dealer for his work in the community. In 2012, he also received the Community Hero Award, North Coast Nurses Association. In 2016, he was inducted into the Cleveland International Hall of Fame, one of 7 inductees out of over 150 nominees. He was also honored by Cleveland City Council in 2016 for his over 41 years of service to the community.

Brother Samad has continued his tireless work on behalf of the youth of Cleveland, speaking in the schools, community and religious institutions, always having time to just talk to them and provide a listening ear and guidance with their problems. He continues to be in demand as a trainer for police, school officials, and the community in issues of gang prevention and intervention and non-violent crisis intervention and mediation. He has continued to embody and work for the principles of Peace in the Hood in his daily life: Peace, Justice and Empowerment.

"The Coalition for a Better Life, Peace in the Hood is happy and enthusiastic to lend support to the Our Young Voices Initiative. Inspiring our young people must be a priority in these turbulent times."

Khalid Samad

Highlights from Real Money, Real World

This wonderful program was presented over a 3 day period. Attendees learned about bank accounts, payroll deductions, and basic finance. For the final day, attendees drew a character. The badge told them their education level, their pay, where they work and how many children they had. They were given a sheet and had to arrange all basic necessities by going to stations that were manned by volunteers. The rules were simple: they could not live with relatives, relatives could not keep their children, and all had a spouse or significant other who was job hunting and could not keep the children. Some had to get a second or a third job. One station was a "chance" station that may be good news or bad news, just like life. Here are a few scenes from the program at our facility.

The first stop for many was the day care and clothing station. Here Sister Karima goes over their options.

Sister Y-Von manned the food station. She took this time to talk about saving money by raising some of your own food, even in an apartment.

Brother Kerby talks about communications options while Brother Greg talks about second jobs.

Brother Khalid goes over transportation options for the youth.

Brother Michael lets a youth draw a card from the "chance" pile

Our Young Voices

Sister Veronica mans the insurance table.

Youth busily figure out their budget.

Youth sometimes had to come back and "renegotiate"

Youth check their budgets to make sure they visited every station.

Our Young Voices

Brother Greg, the volunteers and the youth de brief.

Our youngest camper seems glad someone else is responsible for her "real money, real world"

Painting with the Police, Safety Forces & the Community
*ARTS4PEACE
SAVE THE DATE: MAY 21, 2016 (SATURDAY)
Noon - 3:00 pm
(SATURDAY)

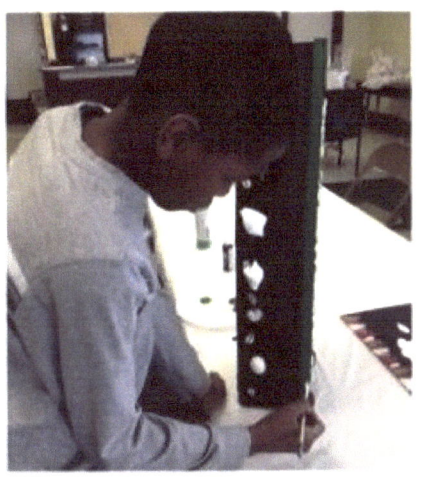

(Acrylic Painting for Chief Calvin Williams
Artist and Entrepreneur: Malikah Abdul Haqq)

ARTS4PEACE
Paint with the Police
and Safety Forces
"YOU'RE INVITED"
Create Art for Peace
Join our UNITY CIRCLE
BRING THE FAMILY
THE COMMUNITY
IS NEEDED!!!

WHERE:
13512 KINSMAN RD
YORK RITE HALL
Time: Noon - 3:00 pm
Contact: Khalid Samad (216) 538-4043
Raja Ali
Office: 216.307-6117
99treasures@gmail.com
FB: peaceinthehood

At 12 noon on May 21, The Coalition for a Better life opened its doors to the community and law enforcement to come together in a neutral environment to build understanding and tear down the walls that divide. The Coalition quickly had 53 attendees. The event was set up so that people could come and go as needed, which made a group picture of the entire group a little more challenging. The youngest attendee was three years old and the oldest attendee refused to divulge her age. The Coalition welcomed law enforcement representatives for the Cleveland Police Department Fourth District, Cleveland Clinic Police, CMSD Police, and CMHA Security.

The Coalition also welcomed the wonderful Margaret Bernstein from WKYC who brought donations of books for the youth attendees to bring home. Special thanks and acknowledgement to Lynn Hampton, president of Black Shield Police Organization. Thanks also to Councilman Zack Reed for his attendance and support and our collaborating partners from the York Rite Masonic Temple, Concerned Citizens, 99 Treasures International, as well as several block clubs in the area.

Attendees agreed that there should be events like this each month. There will be a follow up meeting to discuss implementation, with different groups in the community hosting the event. Please enjoy the pictures from the event.

(Our attendees pose for a group picture!)

(Khalid Samad and Jawaad Mumphrey former CMSD Officer)

Our Young Voices

(Some of our young attendees)

(The finished product)

(Sister Vickie Taylor holds up her purchases)

(Sister Raja Ali and Peace in the Hood Board member Nafisa Abdul Rahim, Ph.D.)

Our Young Voices

(Margaret Bernstein of WKYC)

(Building community relationships
P.O. Marvin Young)

(Brother Khalid Samad, Officer Marvin Young, Officr Scott Floyd and Officer Derrick Dark of Cleveland Clinic PD)

(Mr. Jefferson Tufts of the York Rite Temple trying his hand at painting)

Our Young Voices

(CEO Khalid Samad tries his hand at painting)

(Left to Right, Brother Nate Muhammad, Officer Scott Floyd, Officer Derrick Dark of Cleveland Clinic PD, Brother Khalid Samad, Officer Marvin Young, Brother from Mosque 18, and in front, Margaret Bernstein and Councilman Zack Reed)

(Representatives of the 4th District Community Relations)

(Sister Raja and Sister Aaminah Myles help our young attendees)

Our Young Voices

(Attendees work on painting)

(Officers work on their painting)

Cleveland Scholarship Week 2017

(The finished product)

(Sister Aaminah Myles helps attendees)

Our Young Voices

(Officers sign their name on a painting)

(Margaret Bernstein signs the group painting)

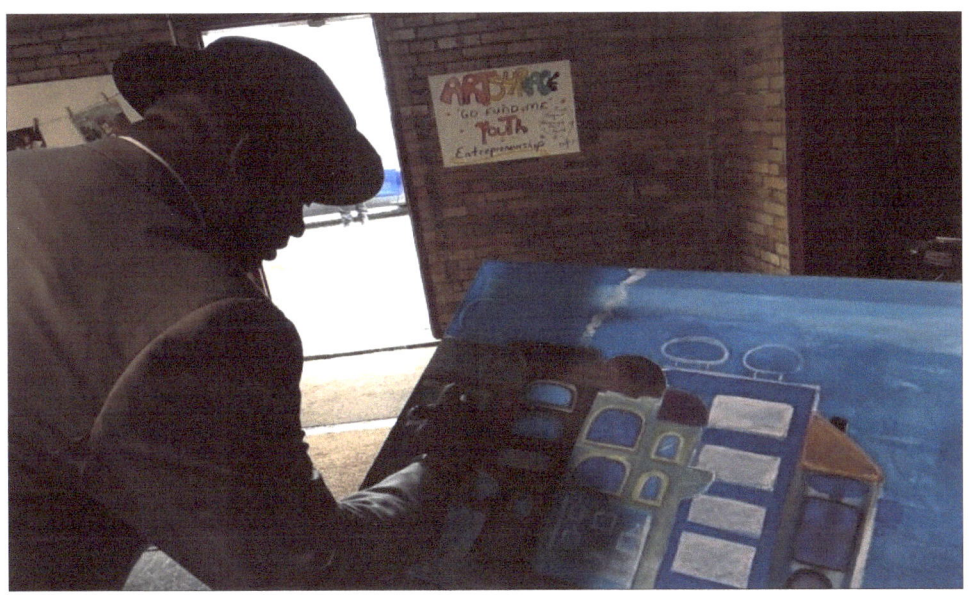

(Nate Muhammad signs the original painting)

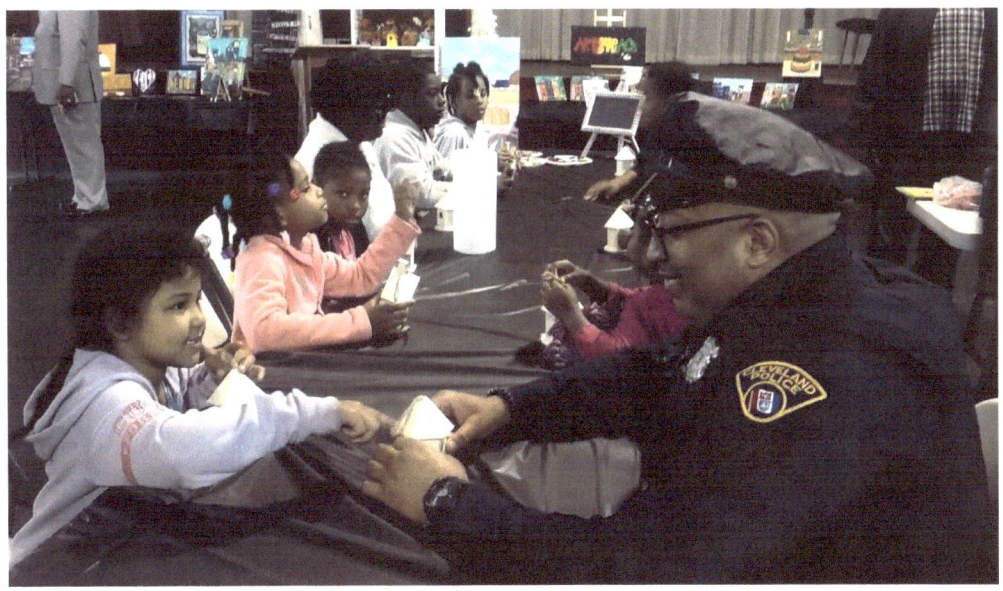

(Painting with a new friend)

Our Young Voices

(Margaret Bernstein and the youth with their books)

(Jamaal Myles)

(Original Painting by Raja Ali)

(CEO Khalid Samad and Detective Lynn Hampton, President of Black Shield)

Our Young Voices

This is the symbol for the principle of Umoja (Unity in the Community)

We hope you enjoyed seeing these pictures! We had a great time! We hope to see everyone out for our next event!

MWM "20" Cleveland Community Organizing and "Speak Out" Session

Social: millionwomanmarch20.com

When: Saturday, August 5, 2017

Time: 2:00pm – 4:30pm

Where: Garfield Heights Library – Room B
5409 Turney Rd, Cleveland, OH 44125

Why: Planning and Organizing Meeting for the Original Million Woman March "20" Year Anniversary Reunion

Theme "Raising up the Mother of Civilization"

We will discuss the issues of Violence and Abuse of Black Women/Girls; Gentrification and Social Engineering in Black Communities; Brothers in Support Cleveland Unit; ARTIVISTS; and Open for Business Proposals

Forming subcommittees:
Programming, Fundraising, Communications, Security, Transportation

Hosted by Cleveland MWM-UM Committee | Email: clevelandmwm20@gmail.com | Contact: 440-703-0030
Join and support at www.millionwomanmarch20.com

Our Young Voices

Our Young Voices

JOIN US FOR END OF CAMP CELEBRATION 2017!

When: July 27, 2017
11:00 am-1 pm
Where: York Temple Building
13512 Kinsman
Cleveland, Ohio

Come hear what our children have learned and see what they have done!

For more information: Please call Sister Raj 216-618-8806 or the offices of Peace in the Hood at (216) 307-6117

 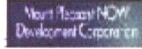   

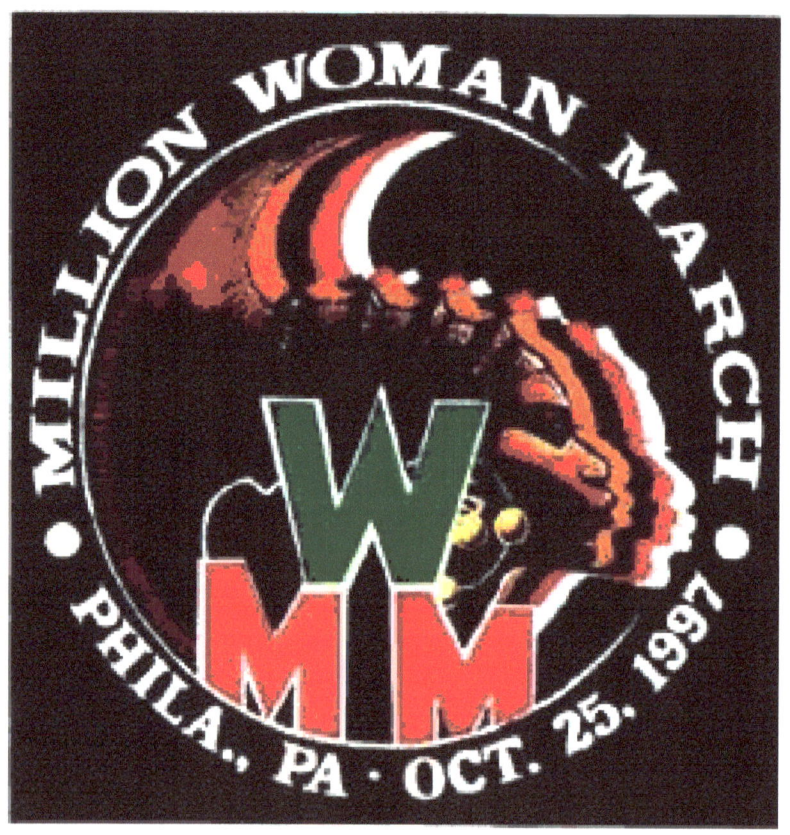

Take the Book Phone Challenge!

Smart is Cool!

Round 1
Boxing. Fitness. Life.

Boxer and ordained minister the Rev. Morris Eason has a passion for helping both kids and adults overcome life's many struggles through a "proven regimen of boxing, training and life coaching." He wholeheartedly supports the Our Young Voices Initiative.

"Morris Eason, a former boxer who once beat "Boom Boom" Mancini. Eason, who often competes in regional tough-man contests, combines the manners of a church deacon -- he's an ordained minister -- with the look of a hit man: bald head, bulging pecs, jaw as square as a sock hop."

Scene Magazine, October 23, 2002

ROUND 1 MINISTRIES
Motivational Speaking, Fitness & Life Coaching

8490 Kinsman road, Novelty, Ohio 44072 • P.O. Box 23474 • Chagrin Falls, OH 44022
P 216.978.6919 • P 440-708-4376 • morris.eason@yahoo.com

Hello,
My Name is Rev. Morris Eason, former Regional Toughman Champion and World Toughman Sweet 16 Finalist. My passion in life is helping kids and families to overcome life's many struggles. Through a proven regimen of boxing, training and life coaching, I can help. If you want to travel down a new path, please contact me right away!

Motivational Speaking

My motivational speeches are geared to inspire audience members to make a change in their lives. Through my personal stories, derived from over 30 years of being in the "Ring," I hope everyone will feel my passion and energy and leave empowered to impact their lives in a positive manner. My fees start at $500 for an event, plus expenses.

One-On-One and Group Fitness Training

There is no other workout like that of a boxer. Minute for minute, a boxer's routine teaches agility, endurance, conditioning and coordination. I conduct daily one hour group boxing fitness sessions consisting of 4 people in a class in addition to scheduled private one-on-one individual lessons. My fees are $15 for the group and $50 for individual sessions.

Counseling: Bullying, Self Esteem, Confidence & Drug Addiction

Bullying, face to face as well as on the internet, and the resulting emotional distress, has become one of the most prevalent problems in today's schools. Kids looking to cope with pressures and family issues often believe that drugs or alcohol will medicate that pain but they soon learn its not the answer. My unique method of combining training, self confidence and personal communication has proven to help these youngsters pull their lives back together. Initial sessions are free. Thereafter, individual sessions are $50 per hour.

Prison Ministry

A record number of kids and young adults are being incarcerated into our prison systems. Often these inmates lose hope and harden their hearts. Through my weekly visits, I have been able to give them a renewed hope and a purpose for living again. Many stays in jail are temporary and these young lives need a ray of hope in dealing with their futures. That's exactly what I do. My services are free. Donations are appreciated.

ROUND 1
Boxing. Fitness. Life.

The 2016 AAMA Annual Scholarship Week Banquet
Cleveland, Ohio

The Banquet was held Thursday, September 8, 2016. The Annual Scholarship Banquet and Community Service Awards Reception was honored to have the support of both City of Cleveland Councilman, Kevin Conwell, and Mrs. Yvonne Conwell, Cuyahoga County Council Representative. The event took place at the Tudor Arms Hotel.

Special Guest Speakers for the evening were Mike Tobin, Public Information Officer, U.S. Attorney from the United States Attorney's Office for the Northern District of Ohio. Also, Felton Thomas, Director of the Cleveland Public Library.

Distinguished invited guests included Mr. and Mrs. Carl S. Ewing, President of the Association of the African American Cultural Garden and others.

Other highlights included a Community Service Award presentation to the following individuals who have dedicated their life to work and service in the community:

> Derrick Polk – Polk played basketball with Ohio State University and The Harlem Globe Trotters as well as playing overseas.
>
> Emanuel Leaks – Leaks played basketball for six pro seasons with four different ABA teams and a pair of NBA clubs. In 2004 Leaks was also Inducted into the Greater Cleveland Sports Hall Of Fame.

(Mike Tobin, U.S. Attorney's Office top right, bottom)

Cleveland Scholarship Week 2017

(Felton Thomas, Director of the Cleveland Public Library)

(State of Ohio Representative, 12th District, John Barnes, Jr. top left)

(Lynn Hampton, President, Black Shield)

(Emanuel Leaks, former pro player, ABA and NBA basketball)

Cleveland Scholarship Week 2017

(Derrick Polk, former Globe Trotter and overseas basketball player)

Our Young Voices

(Cierra Kelley, Cleveland School District top; Sonja Saalam, bottom)

(Ms. Davis, Cleveland Public Library, top; Basheer Jones, bottom)

Our Young Voices

(Kevin Conwell & Footprint Band)

Cleveland Scholarship Week 2017

(Kevin Conwell & Footprint Band)

(Yvonne Conwell, Cuyahoga County Representative, top middle, bottom left)

Cleveland Scholarship Week 2017

(Kevin Conwell, Cleveland City Councilman, top right, bottom right)

Our Young Voices

(Carl and Lavita Ewing, President and Development Chairperson, The Association of African American Cultural Gardens)

(E.B. Smith, Media Associate for the African American Music Association Vice President, E.B. Smith Project LLC, top ,middle; bottom right)

Our Young Voices

Cleveland Scholarship Week 2017

Our Young Voices

(Kent & Angelica WERE 1490)

The 2016
Infinite Scholars College Fair
Cleveland, Ohio

The African American Music Association invited high school students and their families to a "FREE" scholarship fair held September 9, 2016. The Infinite Scholars College Scholarship Fair was held at the Martin Luther King, Jr., Cleveland Public Library located at 1962 Stokes Blvd, Cleveland, Ohio 44106.

Cleveland Scholarship Week 2017

Our Young Voices

Cleveland Scholarship Week 2017

Our Young Voices

(Anthony Battaglia, Cleveland Metropolitan School District)

(Cierra Kelley, Cleveland Metropolitan School District)

(Yvonne Conwell, Cuyahoga County Representative)

Cleveland Scholarship Week 2017

(Kevin Conwell, Cleveland City Councilman)

(Winston Gragg, President of the AAMA, top left; bottom, middle. Lynn Hampton, President, Black Shield, top right)

Cleveland Scholarship Week 2017

(Jean Wilson, Executive Administrator, AAMA, top right, bottom 2nd from left. Kent & Angelica, WERE 1490)

Cleveland Scholarship Week 2017

Major Collaborators & Supporters

Cleveland Scholarship Week 2017

INFINITE SCHOLARS
"The Possibilities are Infinite"

Our Young Voices

Cleveland Scholarship Week 2017

Our Young Voices

Our Young Voices

Cleveland Scholarship Week 2017

Participating Universities and Colleges

Our Young Voices

The University of Akron
Army ROTC

Cleveland Scholarship Week 2017

Cleveland Scholarship Week 2017

Our Young Voices

Our Young Voices

Cleveland Scholarship Week 2017

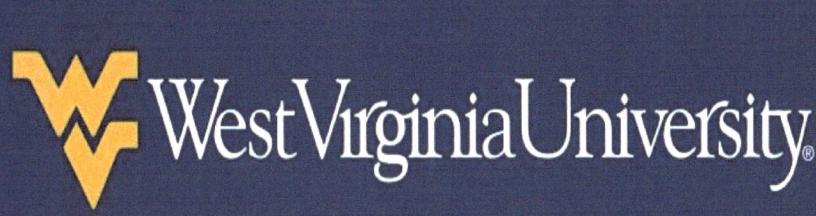

Youngstown
STATE UNIVERSITY

Our Young Voices

Cleveland Scholarship Week
Summary Report

Cleveland Student Attendance in 2012 was 64 students and attendance in 2013 was 122 students.

Cleveland - (September 12, 2014)

Students	141
Parents/Teachers	19
Colleges	21
Awards	$705,000

Cleveland - (September 11, 2015)

Students	235
Parents	31
Colleges	24
Awards	$1,224,350

Cleveland - (September 09, 2016)

Students	160
Parents	31
Colleges	32
Awards	$2,000,000

Our Young Voices

A Proud Supporter of:

Our Young Voices is a Pride in Authorship Initiative publication. The young authors selected have successfully conveyed their thoughts, dreams, and concerns by the written word. They deserve to be celebrated!

2016 Cleveland, Ohio Chapter Scholarship Week
Banquet
College Fair
Our Young Voices Dream Contest

Our Young Voices

INFINITE ∞ SCHOLARS

"The Possibilities are Infinite"

During the past decade, the Infinite Scholars Program has served more than 100,000 students and has facilitated more than 1 Billion Dollars in scholarships and financial aid.

Infinite Scholarship Fairs are located in 27 cities and growing. We connect students with scholarship and financial aid opportunities from participating colleges. There is no cost to students or colleges to attend our fairs.

Nearly 300 colleges and universities annually participate in our scholarship fairs. Each fair hosts between 50 and 100 colleges. Our Featured Colleges provide Infinite Scholars with additional support beyond attending our scholarship fairs.

http://www.infinitescholar.org/

Cleveland Scholarship Week 2017

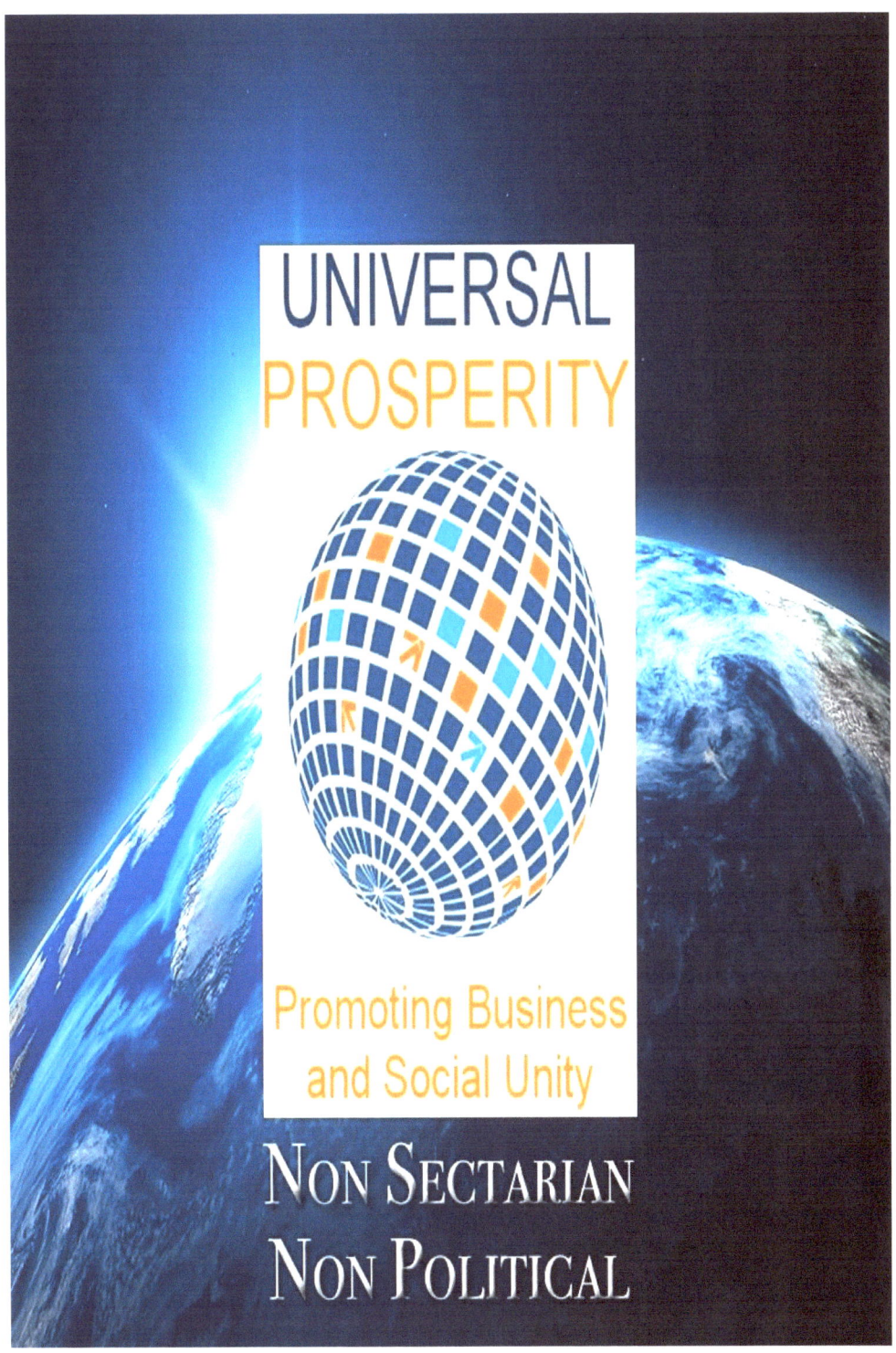

Supporters of Our Young Voices can get their books published on Amazon.com for only $249 and get 10 free copies!

Mention "Our Young Voices" on the "Contact Us" Page or VIA E-Mail

Easy Self-Publishing

http://uptownmediaventures.com

(Click the Publishing Page)

Forward E-Mail Inquiries to:

uptownliterary@gmail.com

Join our Nationwide Network!

Our Young Voices

2017

Scholarship Week

Cleveland, Ohio

Banquet
College Fair
Our Young Voices Contest

www.ingramcontent.com/pod-product-compliance
Lightning Source LLC
Chambersburg PA
CBHW041509220426
43661CB00047B/1518